CONVERSATIONS FROM THE LEFT, RIGHT, & HEART

A Collection of Poetic Writing

To Caitlin,

Thank you so, so much for your support! It means a lot! I hope you enjoy the book.

Best,
Haylo

CONVERSATIONS FROM THE LEFT, RIGHT, & HEART

A Collection of Poetic Writing

AMS Golden

Columbus, Ohio

Conversations from the Left, Right, & Heart

Published by Gatekeeper Press
2167 Stringtown Rd, Suite 109
Columbus, OH 43123-2989
www.GatekeeperPress.com

Library of Congress Control Number: 2020951089

ISBN (paperback): 9781662907890
eISBN: 9781662907906

Dedications

To my soulmate, my flame, and my best friend,

Thank you for finding me. You have inspired me when nothing else could anymore. You brought light and color back into my life. This would never have been possible without you. I know you'll recognize yourself in much of my writing; you are a beautiful muse and an even more beautiful person.

To my sisters, blood and soul,

Thank you for being my strength and my reason to never, ever give up in life. You are all things beautiful and right. You are my human life vests.

To my Spunky, specifically, you are the reason I wrote and still write. I hope this makes you as proud of me as I have been proud of you.

&

To my wonderful husband,

Thank you for trusting me and encouraging me to "just do it." Your support in all my work endeavors has never gone unnoticed. You are truly appreciated and I hope you know I don't take it or you for granted. I don't know how I'd have gotten through the last few years without you. You are a saint!

Contents

Conversations from the Left, Right, and Heart

I feel like I can't breathe. The air feels too thick to fit down my throat. Heart begins to panic and wonders if it needs to run on its last reserve. I don't know how to answer it, because I've never been more afraid.

Right Brain tells me to relax, that it's just the years of unsaid words filling my lungs. It's becoming too heavy to hold onto and she's ready to let go. The words are waiting to be released, waiting to be breathed out, waiting to be heard – waiting to be seen like the first breath of winter.

I am the winter. I am dark. I am unforgiving. I am brutal. My cold front is impenetrable. Without seeking shelter somewhere else, you'll surely die with me.

Shouldn't have had those cigarettes today. Left Brain, my old friend, kicks Right Brain down. *You didn't take your pill yet today. You should do that.* I could go grab my water and do as it says, but I don't actually want to get up. I sat down here because I *wanted* to get things off my chest. It's getting so hard to breathe.

Heart grips me tightly and whispers, "I'm scared." I think he's causing a heart attack.

I'm coughing up full sentences now—statements that I should be telling you, but I can't. I can't face you right now. *Just push it all down until the urge is gone.* Left Brain always knows what to say to keep the raw emotions at bay. Left Brain wants me to be angry, wants me to continue to ignore you, wants me to hurt you. *After five years you deserve to be angry.*

I know I have the right to feel angry, but then I feel guilty. Heart always bleeds for you when I'm the one hurting. Why do I care if my feelings somehow bother you? I'm entitled to my feelings. This would be so much easier if I hated you.

Right Brain sings to me. *Breathe out the dust of long-shrouded feelings—let them flow.* Left Brain doesn't like this. Left Brain is shouting about the many times the flowing of words became the flowing of tears and he hates tears. He doesn't want me to give in. He slaps Right Brain across her cheek and scolds her. Right Brain turns away like a wounded child. Why did Right Brain have to be my trauma? Why did we always have to hide her?

Heart begins sobbing—he hates seeing his parents fight.

We're both your trauma, crazy girl.

Left Brain is smart. Left Brain is everything I ever wanted to be—intelligent, rational, grounded . . . . Right Brain is so beautiful though. I could never give her up. I'd never find someone like her again.

We're going to heal. Don't worry.

She is light. She is daydreams and what-ifs. She is every fragrance of flower and every fragment of hope I have left. I wish my words did her justice. The way she shines ....

Cut it out. You want to heal? Stop touching the wound. Damn you, Left Brain. Always politically, cynically correct.

Just one? Can we feel one? Heart begs to be heard. He begs to just let out a little pain – to ease his load. He's suffocating; turning blue.

One – you can feel one. Left Brain is very begrudging.

I don't think Left Brain has ever admired me as much as I admired him. Left Brain thinks I'm foolish because I always let Right Brain and Heart complete just enough of their transactions to remind him that I'm a human with emotions. I try to remind him daily there isn't really a switch to *stop* feeling, but he thinks I'm being naïve. He tells me going back to my doctor and accepting their medication would "flip the switch."

I tell Heart I'm ready. He whispers to Right Brain who takes out her pen.

Go ahead, girl. We're listening.

Arrival Time—10:15 a.m.

Time keeps telling me I must turn back;

I feel like a train running off the tracks.

Heartache, deceit—it's all another game.

Winning seems so easy when you can block out all the pain.

Love Tastes a Lot Like Arsenic

So here I am in a pool of blood at your feet. Feed me more poison. Make this sick love taste sweet.

Celestial Cheating

And you made me feel like the sun in your sky,
But I found you gazing at the stars each night ...

Taking Notes

Our arguments mean little and our apologies fall frail.
Your words become my weapons every time you fail.

Last Will and Testament

You don't get to show up at my funeral when you're the one who buried me.

Behind the Mask

She's so done trying; every day is spent crying as she lies again to herself.

So she sits alone in the darkness because who could have thought this?

No one knows how messed up she feels or how hurt.

I Adore You

I want to be everything you never imagined was real;
I want to be the reason you can still feel ...

Crossing That Line

So I guess these are just my racing thoughts, and as always they have run a marathon back to you.

The Boy Bands Hit Harder When You Grow Up

Some 98° and some alcohol later, I have to admit, the hardest thing I ever had to do was pretend that I don't love you, even though I do.

What Burns More: Death Valley, the Arctic Plateau, or Your Pride?

And so you sit on the hot coals to prevent your emotional numbness from freezing your heart. You can't feel the burn anymore, but I'm sure you can taste the salted pain from your eyes on your tongue.

Floundering

I think I liked you better before you said you loved me. We didn't have to work so hard then to be better than "all right then." Used to spend hours on the phone and now it's like we lost our voice to Aphrodite's crone. But you aren't the Little Mermaid and our words can still flow free, so why is it when I look at you, you no longer speak?

Let's Play Freeze-Tag

I wish the world could stop and freeze every time you say "Fuck you" to me.... Maybe then you'll finally see how often you're losing me ....

Cobwebs in the Attic Part 1 (*Spring Cleaning with a Struggling "Artist"*)

I wish I had beautiful words to write you so you would know how you cleaned the spiderwebs from my mind and turned on the lights; how your love shone like a prism, casting rainbows even into the night. But I'm bad at poetry, so this is the best you'll get: I love you.

Damned from Birth

You are the closest thing to love that I'll ever feel and the closest to heaven I'll ever be.

"Winter is Coming"

Zooey and JGL got *(500) Days of Summer*, but I would take even one night of winter if it meant I got ....

> *"... to die by your side; well the pleasure,*
> *the privilege is mine ..."*[1]

Honey is Sweet, but You're Sweeter

Let's play a game ....

In this game, you can be a flower and I'll be a bumblebee.
Let me crawl inside your dark center and remind you that
even this far from sunlight, you're still so vital to me.

You 101

You're like an intricate piece of art, like a relic or ancient scroll, that no one else has discovered exists, but I've had the greatest privilege of stumbling upon you in these ruins. You're in a language I don't know. Not yet. I can't explain you, to myself or anyone. But I'll learn you. I'll study; stay up all night, until I have my Ph.D. in *You*.

Cobwebs in the Attic Part 2

I haven't written in years. I kept a journal most of my life, but if I opened it now, spiders would crawl out of it. (Real spiders. Not imaginary ones on the wall ....) I know in my last entry, I scrawled your name and how you made me rethink love. I started to write to you, but it seemed sad. Not sad in that sense you may never read it, but because I realized, I spend so many hours talking to you, that when my clock strikes 19 and you're falling asleep alone in your bed, my only thoughts are then wanting to be with you. But how many letters can someone write where the only words are, "I crave to be wrapped up in your arms, listening to your breath slow down and your pulse steady as your arms get heavy and I kiss you goodnight"? Well, the answer is a dozen. But you make me want to write. Paint. Sit at the piano for hours. Not to escape anything anymore, but to feel again. You brought light back into my life. Color, too. (Even if rainbows still confuse me ....) And I promise one day to repay you for that—to thank you properly. Whether it be when you get off the "huge, horrifying plane" or when you ask me to save you from ever getting on a plane. I'm going to make sure you know that I meant every word I ever said to you. I'm going to make sure you know you are loved. Unconditionally. For making me smile. For making me hope. For making me feel. For making me laugh. For never walking away. For never giving up. For loving me, as much as I love you.

You Were Supposed to be a Mosaic (*Sorry I Suck at Art*)

I'll give you pieces of me to fill the broken parts of you. But how can I be of value to you after there becomes nothing left of me?

AMS Golden

My Favorite Shape is You

Pixel by pixel I once traced along your frame;

Memorizing every inch of you the way I've memorized your name.

I count the time left until I can feel your skin beneath my fingers for even just one day;

I swear when the moment comes I'll even try to memorize the way you taste.

EKG

For someone who feels so dead inside, you sure make my heart beat

faster

harder ....

Who needs a stress test when you can fall in love?

The Luxury of Love

Our home is unnecessarily large. We remind ourselves we are so rich that we have a dozen airliners in our backyard. We have double gates for double security and only employ the best guards with the strongest K-9. To us, the sky is our limit.

But soon we'll stop living in airports and our feet will stand firmly on the ground. We will find a cozy little house with a tree in the backyard. We'll paint a white picket fence and rescue a puppy. One day our home will be *one place*.

The Deep End

I know you feel like you're drowning, but I promise to risk breaking my neck out in the tide to rescue you, if you promise to just keep swimming.

AMS Golden

Semester Abroad

I used to live in the past, unable to picture a future.

This love at a distance is hard to explain, but worth trying to find an answer.

Would things be any easier if we had just met in college?

I guess it doesn't really matter ....

Because of you I finally have a reason to wake up tomorrow.

Classic Love

The night we met had a "Whole Lotta Love" and a little Led Zeppelin. And I admitted in the morning that classic rock wasn't much my thing, but you smiled and said it was all right. I knew then I'd watch Jimmy Page paint a wall if it meant I would see you smile like that again.

A Golden Book

They said Prince Charming was a fairy tale and that good
men don't exist,

But everyone I meet admits I married a golden prince.

Alcohol You in the Morning

You were my first and likely last drunk text and it left me confused. If I'm drinking to forget and that whole evening is a blur, then how come I still remembered you?

Bestseller

Once upon a time, we were on the same page.

Now we aren't even reading the same book.

We used to be my favorite story.

You and I were the best.

The end.

Ex's and Oh's

An ex-boyfriend once told me, "Promises are made to be broken." I hated him for it.

Now I think they are the only true words he ever said.

Campfire Story

The night we kissed felt like morphine lips and a Novocain tongue, dancing like the trees at the campground; your fingers numbing pain like lidocaine and burning my skin down to the bone. The relief you gave was temporary. I was broken in ways you couldn't understand. My demons were my soulmates and I couldn't let you in. I would call you "tiger," watching you pounce on life with wild desire. But I should've known your hunt for me would end real soon, for I was the weakest of all your prey. Only vultures feed on dying things and you needed life to feed your ways.

> *I never hated you for what you did.*
> *I wish you well.*

"That's Meta"

Crying in the shower during a storm begins to seem pretty meta when you're trying to think about anything other than reasons for why you are crying in a shower during a storm.

I Always Wanted a Brother

Do we have a song? I don't know. So I've listened to them all.

Someone sees my internet history and wonders if I'm going through a breakup or if I'm planning on ending it all.

EMTs show up with alcohol and chocolate ...

And a straight-jacket.

They lock me up before feeding me a shot of gin.

> *Big Brother*—there when no one else is ....[2]

Once a Martyr, Now a Saint

It's amazing. How in love I once felt with you. Like you created heaven and Earth and I would kill myself trying to move them to bring us closer. And now look at us. After all these years. The distance hasn't changed but we haven't been this far apart since the day you created light in my life. But I guess most people never really know their God.

AMS Golden

Words are Cheaper than Tickets

He sends me words and flowers to occupy the time and space until he can send himself, but words get forgotten over time, and even the most beautiful flowers wilt without care.

The Left is Right and The Right is Wrong Part 1

My left and right brain are at war with each other. I think they are getting a divorce. The Left tells the Right it cries too much, feels too much, that it's too heavy. The Right tells the Left it's insensitive, cold. It tells the Left that it's tried to lose weight, but it's hard to let go of the body of the one you love, even when it's dead weight; even when you're tired.

The Left has left the room again, leaving me with the Right's thoughts ....

I hope the Left gets to keep the house in the end.

Broken Hearts Taste Like Whiskey

My coffee tastes like whiskey and my skin feels like paper.

I want to rip you from my heart,

Like a child rips petals from a flower when it asks, "Does he love me ...?"

He loves me not.

The knot in my stomach makes me sick;

Even my bile tastes like whiskey.

It's 12 p.m. and my body flows with more alcohol so my lips begin to taste of whiskey to forget the taste of you.

An Entire Country Tainted by You
(*You Don't Know Your Power*)

"Sad Songs"—Thanks *Amazon*!

"The system says I want this, but I don't."[3]

I *want* to be okay. Where can I purchase "Okay"? How much will it cost me? Would you like to have a copy? Maybe we could share.

I've got the cost covered if you can translate it on your own.

> *Remember when we made each other okay?*

What Was Ours?

If *you* had Secondhand Serenade ...

Do we have it *Third*hand?

Or are we the sound of silence so loud

We're screaming?

> *"Call, I'm desperate for your voice ...."*[4]

Screaming into the Reactor

You and I don't put in the same amount of energy into us anymore ....

You're sound energy: pretty words, empty words, words that fall weak.

I'm a nuclear power plant and I'm about to melt down.

Soon there'll be nothing left of me to give to you.

AMS Golden

You Stained Me

My teeth are stained from the years of holding your name in my mouth, shouting it at the stars, and wishing someday you'd come true.

Life Lesson

I never knew how to apologize until I met you. Now I feel sorry for everything.

Even for this.

AMS Golden

My King of Cups

Sometimes I look at you and it's like the first time I've seen your face all over again, and then you open your mouth and your heart pours out, and I have to sit back and wonder how more people have not wanted to throw themselves at your feet, and how the hell with all who did, did I become the one you want.

Self-Destruct in 10, 9, 8 ...

Bloody knuckles and bloodshot eyes,

Tears running down my face and blood running down my thigh,

I can't even look at myself.

Tell me, am I still beautiful to you?

Tell me, is my body still perfection?

Tell me, can you still want this mess?

Tell me.

Please, tell me.

Can you tell me we're okay?

AMS Golden

Refractions

Kaleidoscope eyes that see only in black and white,

I want to make your life bright.

Shattered heart that bleeds and aches,

This time I want to make things right.

The Truth About Stars

Most people don't realize the stars we see, the stars we call beautiful, the stars we trust with our deepest wishes are already dead when we notice their light. Maybe that means there's potential for me to still be valued, even if it takes until death.

To the World, You'll Be Sorry. — Unapologetically Yours

In a world where you can be anything, choose to be alive.

And if the world tells you that who you are should die,

I give you permission to blacken both its eyes.

A world that can't see your potential deserves not to see at all.

~~Pieces~~ Peace

Her ghost still haunts me – a relationship unfinished and never even started. I'd let her go, exorcise this body, but I don't remember how to be me without her shadow hanging over my shoulder. I'm scared to one day forget her. I'm just one piece in the infinity without her, but I know it's time I let her …

Rest in Peace.

AMS Golden

Homesick for the Unknown

I never touched you, but you held my hand through my hardest days.

I never kissed you, but I felt the warmth of your breath at my loneliest moments.

I never met you, but I fell in love with you with such a brazen desire to know you better than myself.

I never got to know you, but I haven't felt at home since that day you entered my life.

The Heart Remembers

You remind me of soft-serve ice cream, sparkling in rainbow sprinkles, on the brightest summer day. You remind me of the first snowflake of the year, spotted dancing past the window while I'm daydreaming in class. You remind me of sidewalk chalk drawings that felt like works of Picasso, and pride from strangers smiling at them passing by. You remind me of jumping in leaves, sending them flying like confetti, celebrating the ending of one year and falling into another. You remind me of a happiness that I could only feel as a child, blissfully unaware of the harsh reality of this world. I hope I never forget this feeling.

The New World

In the darkness of the night, I want to memorize your skin,

Name the canyon of your navel and the peaks of your hips like national parks and wonders of the world.

I want to mark off destinations I've seen with love bites,

Plant kisses where I'll revisit time and again.

Neck, throat, lips ....

I want to get married in your eyes and honeymoon between your thighs;

I'll make a home in your chest and together we'll let the light in so you can see all I have come to love in you.

Uranium Sulfide (US$_2$)

I don't know much about chemistry, but you make me want to understand what we have.

So I've begun to study and I've found that ...

chem·is·try
/ˈkeməstrē/

Is a noun that means:

1. the branch of science that deals with the identification of the substances of which matter is composed; the investigation of their properties and the ways in which they interact, combine, and change; and the use of these processes to form new substances.

2. the complex emotional or psychological interaction between two people.

I learned that the chemicals are elements, pure until mixed and conjoined.

I learned elements are identified by their color,

Like the way your eyes match the leaves we watch change shades as time goes by;

Mass,

Like the weight of your mere existence in my life;

Volume,

Like the sound of your voice when you whisper to me in the dark veil of night;

Length,

Like your fingers slowly running down my spine;

Malleability,

Like the way you bend like branches in a storm to calm the hurricane inside me;

Melting point,

Like the moment you told me you're not leaving this time;

Hardness,

Like your anger or my stubbornness when we just cannot agree;

Odor,

Like the smell of your shampoo or your breath against my skin in the morning;

Temperature,

Like the warmth of your body beside me in bed.

I learned that elements are matter and matter is anything that takes up space.

And you matter;

And you do, in my heart, in my head, in my dreams, in my bed ....

I learned that matter can change form though, but through all of these changes, the same amount of matter exists before and after the change—nothing is created or destroyed.

And I believe after all this time, we can adapt to our changes too;

We cannot be destroyed either.

I want to occupy this space and time together.

Bond with me like hydrogen and oxygen—rain on me. Let's become something stronger than either one of us alone.

I don't know about you, but I think scientists would call what we have "chemistry."

End Game

There are no glowing EXIT signs in life;

No one tells you when the house is on fire, just how to escape without a burn;

Crash landings don't come with oxygen or floatation devices;

Falling face-first in love or in a ditch both leave you wounded;

And the earth-shattering tremors at fault lines are always your fault;

There is nothing natural about your disaster, love;

> But over time we all learn to bend and break, regrow and reshape;
>
> One day people will bow to you in respect and talk about how beautiful you were;
>
> One day you will grow flowers from your bones and your soul will attract butterflies;
>
> One day the pressure of this world will threaten to make you as hard as a rock—a diamond;
>
> But oh, love, how you'll shine in the end ....

The Left is Right and The Right is Wrong Part 2

The Left tells the Right not to expect change; old habits *Die Hard*. But the Right reminds the Left that even Bruce Willis surrendered himself for love during *Armageddon*.

You Gave Me Reason to Fear Death

The night I was in the emergency room, I feared the worst, like dying, but what scared me most was the thought of leaving you before we ever met.

Thank you.

Every Story is Beautiful, but Yours is My Favorite

Your story doesn't end here, even if it looks dark now.

You were never meant to be a John Green or Rachel Cohn novel. You are a Chuck Palahniuk, a Bukowski, a Kerouac.... You are all the beauty and chaos that is "bestseller" writing.

You—your story—is beautiful.

You are worth holding on to, just like a favorite book: coffee and cigarette-stained pages, water-damaged, spine broken, pages tucked in to keep from falling out, dog-eared corners of favorite passages, favorite lines marked with ink, and an indent where the fingers touched the page time after time.

You are my favorite story to read and I promise you, I know your story doesn't end here.

Who Does the Dishes Now?

Trust breaks like porcelain when the right person does the wrong thing;

When the right moment is there, but there is nothing left to give.

> *I needed you. Where were you?*
>
> *Now whose hands will bleed?*

Ticket to Ride

How long do we ride the merry-go-round before we admit even the roller coaster was a better ride in our relationship?

Making Lunch

I am spread thin, so smoothly, even PB&J sandwiches are jealous of me now.

My Friend, Sheetrock

Our silence has become so routine that I stopped picking up my phone and began sitting alone in the corners of this room. I began talking to the walls when my thoughts got loud. They always listen quietly and offer me great support.

Life is Just a Hasbro Game...Right?

It's 4 a.m. and as I try to go back to sleep, it dawns on me that no one I know writes about 4 a.m. ....

3 a.m. is the witching hour, the in-love hour, the "I miss you" hour, the how have my eyes not closed yet hour, the waking from this nightmare hour ...

And any hour after 4 a.m. is the daily-grind hour, the time to get up and shower hour, the cup of coffee is still too hot but I must go hour, the 3 mile run before a suit and tie hour, the "I love you" and kiss goodbye hour ...

No one writes about 4 a.m., when your head aches like a back that has supported too much all wrong yesterday and you are paying for it today; and your eyes carry bags so heavy they need to pay extra at the gate; and you toss and turn like a hurricane at sea, or maybe it's just the acid in your gut, which grumbles the truth to you: "You Lost"; and you look at the clock again and it says 4:43 a.m. and you don't know where the time has gone but you realize sleeping now is futile when your alarm clock will ignore that you've been awake all night in an hour's time and just scream at you to repeat this game again tomorrow.

"I Can't Go to the Kitchen Without You"

Since you've been gone, I've made friends with the kitchen;

Drink my coffee alone and make my favorite meals,

The stove tells great jokes and the microwave runs as hot and cold as you,

Haven't broken any dishes lately and washed you from every crevice,

Began leaning on the walls for support and talking to the bottles at the bar in the refrigerator;

I used to think I couldn't enter this room without you...

But I'm learning the oven can provide the warmth I never got from you.

AMS Golden

Are You Afraid of the Light?

I stay up each night because I'm afraid of losing my daily progress and having to start over when I wake up.

TOD: February 2nd

I habitually check the obituaries when I wake up in the morning to assure myself I haven't died yet. I've begun to think of waking up as a fluke. In a few months when it gets cold, I'll crawl underground for warmth like the groundhog. In the spring they'll bring flowers where I should've risen, but chose to stay.

Not Dead Yet

Loving you felt like dying and every day I couldn't wait to take my last breath.

I'll follow you into that good night ....[5]

Still Looking for "Y"

We have so many problems I'm beginning to look at us like a math book: something I was never good with and nothing I'll ever need.

There Must be a Mistake

How do you sleep knowing I'm awake in a bed without you?

Every night without you should be a mistake.

It's Official

Does writing while the world around me sleeps make me
an official artist or make me officially sad?

It took twenty-eight years, but it's official.

Maiden Voyage

I don't remember "ships" before you;

Did I tell them all the things I tell you?

Did I hold crazy expectations for them, just to disappoint me?

Did I talk to them every day and wake at all hours for them?

Did I ever cry for them?

Did I ever tell them I love them?

Did their voice ever sound like coming home?

I hit the iceberg hard with you and

I think I'm drowning and starting to forget;

But I don't *want* to remember a time before you.

AM or PM?

It's 5 o'clock somewhere;

Someone enters the bar for a night of drinking.

It's 5 o'clock somewhere;

Someone is still wide awake thinking.

Methods of Intoxication

Even at your darkest lows, you were still my brightest high. I would inhale you into my lungs, lick you from my fingertips, swallow you down like Jonah and the whale, inject you where it hurt .... One hit and I was addicted, love. No peer pressure ever felt as strong as the weight of your body on mine. You were my drug of choice. And even knowing the pain you caused, knowing how you could ruin my life ... I'd choose you all over again.

Would You Love Me More if I Were Less of an Emotional Whore?

I'm not easy to love.

I shut myself away in a tower I built;

Dropped the ladder from the window so you can't get up;

Cut myself on my own blades.

I'm not easy to love.

I will let you in and then let you down;

Build you up and then cower in your aura;

I am hell and spitfire, with enough venom in my teeth to kill you while tearing your flesh from bone;

I'll tear you apart just to see if you still feel.

I'm not easy to love.

I'll cry and hate myself for all I did to you;

I'll apologize through tears and mean it though you won't believe a word;

I'll punish myself like the mother that threatens "father" and the father that threatens with a belt.

I'm not easy to love.

But I do love you.

AMS Golden

My Lease is Up

I'm losing you.

You say I'm not, but I taste the bitterness in your voice. I feel how cold the bed is in the morning, because you never came in last night. I see the "vacant" sign in your eyes and I know I can be replaced for the right price.

I'm losing you.

Because my words have soured. Because I hid beneath all the blankets and kicked you out of the fort. Because even when I occupied the space in your heart, I never filled you.

I'm losing you.

You say I'm not, but I know because I pushed you away when all I wanted was for you to stay.

Warning: Flammable

Why are we still in love when the air around us smells like burning matches and tastes of carbon monoxide;

when you look black and blue after a day with me and I'm bleeding by the end of a night with you;

when I run to watch you chase me just to see if you still care and you fail to keep your promises to see if I'll wait there?

Why are we still in love when it's so clear we are a hazardous pair?

I think it's because even at our darkest we still explode with such a flare ....

Like Christmas lights.

Like fireworks.

Like the sun before the endless night.

(We can still be beautiful ....)

Language is Archaic

Words.

So many words.

I could write you a novel with all the words in my head,

Yet I'm not convinced you'd read it;

And even if you did, I'm not convinced you'd understand the plot.

Maybe I need to learn new words.

Foreign words, to me.

I could read your dictionary cover to cover;

I could learn proper English from a proper Tudor tutor;

Yet I'm not convinced a single word would make a difference to you anymore.

Words.

So many words.

But somehow there are no words to express how badly I want this to end.

Language is dead. Let me kiss you instead.

A Wish for a Summer Six Hours Apart

We began in months spent haphazardly gazing out on insomnia rivers;

The summer nights were lonely enough to leave me cold and make me shiver.

I used to fear with our declining mental health we were just hallucinations in my head;

But how different would those nights have been if I were sleeping in your bed?

We would talk of where to make a home for one heart built from two that shattered;

Time together moving fast and slow, and nothing but you were all that mattered.

> *We never smoldered slowly like ashes, love,*
> *we were an arson—roaring passion.*

So I started making wishes into the dark of night, and dreaming of wishes coming true from those empathetic, dying orbs of light;

I sometimes wonder before I fall asleep how few you must see instead, as your world is slowly waking to the sun shining in your bed ....

> *How I wish the world could sleep forever and*
> *I could wake up where you lie ....*

I Don't Recognize Her Anymore

I have hated looking at my reflection for so long that when I see myself in photos now, I don't even recognize it's me.

Sometimes, I even think that *girl is pretty* ....

Abandoned House

You brought the matches and I brought the records. We drank until the sun came up. No one had lived here in years and yet we made it feel warm and alive. Should we call this your place or mine? It didn't matter. It doesn't matter. For when the record scratches to a halt and the last flame burns out .... No matter how many steps forward I take, I won't find you in the dark. This love was abandoned years ago and no one lives here now.

Your Brain is Just Sick

You send a card to an aunt who is recovering from a lost battle with arthritic knees. You sit with a friend when she is hit by the news she has an STD. You send flowers to a coworker when she is diagnosed with cancer and then send chocolate when she completes chemo. You check in with your sister who lives with lupus.

So why are people with chemical imbalances left to be so lonely?

If mental illness weren't so taboo, we would sit with each other outside therapy sessions and send flowers at milestone appointments, too.

A person isn't "damaged" or "broken" when held by the hands of anxiety or depression. And a person shouldn't be ignored because they must repeat, *repeat*, **repeat** a routine to feel like they can breathe. And someone who can't shake off a habit that made them forget why they needed to start in the first place shouldn't be condemned.

Cancel "mental illness" and call it what it is—a "disease of the brain." You're not "mental." Your brain is just sick. And you can recover, too.

Love Child

The darkness holds a familiar calm that only nothingness and you can carry;

I'd been thinking I felt at home with you – there was nothing in you that I found scary.

I'd have married you at first sight and built us a home and given you children;

But your fear caused doubt and our time ran out, and our love became something to be hidden.

But our love was born despite this;

Shame she'll grow up before we meet.

What do we get a 7-year-old child that
was dropped off at our feet?

Cobwebs in the Attic Part 3

If I step to the left, I'll have spiders in my hair;

I see them crawling along the walls;

I can feel them burrowing in my skin.

I thought you cleared them out when you moved in.

It was silly to think you'd have done that work;

I was naïve to believe you'd choose to stay.

I used to play up here as a child, every single day.

Started with *Barbies*, coloring books, and board games;

Then it was you, *you*, **you** ....

There was always something new for us to do;

Never lonely or bored for more than a minute,

And always someone there to care.

If I step to the right, I'm back downstairs,

Where someone else is living now,

Keeping the spot I left for you warm.

It's been five long years

And I don't like the spiders

So I decided it was time to stop living alone.

Love in the Time of CoVid

The airports may be closed, but my heart remains open. While our union may be on a display board with the lights spelling out "Delayed," I trust the day I can wrap my arms around you will be right on time.

AMS Golden

Terminal Event

We reached out hands and touched on hearts before we ever touched down on land.

After the Yearbooks are Signed

In grammar school, I was voted "most likely to succeed." Years later, I'm waking in the middle of the night just to try to breathe. I check my bank account like a Magic 8 Ball and ask it if I'll ever get my life back on track. "Ask again later." I cry as much as I eat now, and I eat a lot when I can remember to swallow the lump in my throat.

In high school, my guidance counselor told me I was "average." Years later and I'd be happy to just be "average" again.

Cut Me to the Core

My compassion for second, third, and 800th tries has dropped so low, I dug a hole through the Earth and came out on the other side ....

Now I'm drowning in an ocean
instead of tears for you.

Would You Rather: Be Invisible Forever or Never Be Able to See Again?

I want us to connect. Know something finds us across the distance of lands and oceans, fears and the many years, and that it can hold us together until we can hold each other. And just like I don't ever want to forget the sound of your voice, even through a receiver, I don't want to forget what you look like either. But for years I've been fantasizing about the invisible man. I've made every day Halloween to try to love you harder, even when I can't picture your face or wrap my arms around you. But if I'm being honest, I'd rather be marrying Frankenstein's monster. At least I'd know what I was waking up next to every day.

Paging Dr. Kevorkian

In a dissociative state, is it still suicide or is it considered euthanasia?

Be a Real Boy

It's unfair: the number of unfinished conversations I've had waiting for you and it's rude of you to let your coffee go cold when I made sure I brewed enough for two.

Switching Gears

I need to stop jumping into the car and driving to the airport when I know you haven't even left your house yet.

I need to put this car in reverse, but I was never the best at parking.

Sobering Thought

The last time I drank tequila, I shoved my foot so deep into my mouth it came out my ass and our silence was so awkward crickets could be heard in the busy streets of town.

The last time I drank gin, I laid on my floor wishing I was six feet under and cried into a text message that I didn't know how to be me without you.

The last time I drank Jameson, I was celebrating your freedom and encouraging you to find yourself and start anew, but felt like a failure because I still failed you.

The last time I drank scotch, I was determined to forget you, but the alcohol burned my throat as much as your name burned on the tip of my tongue and I quit.

You see … without you, I'm weak. Without you, I'm all liquor.

I really want to be all right sober.

After Life

When I die, I'm not looking for heaven or to be reincarnated into a bird or a tree. I just hope when I die you won't forget me.

> *I wouldn't be disappointed if we got to redo*
> *life together, the right way, though ....*

What Mirror Did I Break?

I've had seven years of bad luck.

But I only remember breaking my own heart ....

AMS Golden

Past, Present, and Future

I was 11 years old when I realized home wasn't where I was born and 21 years old when I realized home wasn't a place at all.

I was 14 years old when I began to feel alone and empty inside and 16 years old when I began to wish I would die.

I was 18 years old when I realized I wanted to help others feel less alone and 20 years old when I declared myself a psychology major.

I was 27 years old when I was laid off as a counselor and I decided to write down my thoughts over the last 10 years to ease my own troubled thoughts.

I never wanted to be a "writer" but at 28 years old it was all that quieted my mind.

Footnotes

1. Lyrics from "There is a Light That Never Goes Out" by the Smiths.

2. Reference to George Orwell's *1984*.

3. Reference to Marc-Uwe Kling's *Qualityland*.

4. Lyrics from "Your Call" by Secondhand Serenade.

5. Reference to Dylan Thomas's "Do Not Go Gentle into That Good Night."

Author's Note

I used to write for fun for friends and my sister. Fiction. Not even good fiction. Nothing serious.

In college, I began creative writing and journalism classes, and for a split second I thought, "I could do this …." But I let fear and self-doubt keep me from pursuing that dream.

Starting in 2015, I began my career in the social services field for individuals with intellectual and developmental disabilities. While I never stopped writing (for me), it wasn't until I lost my job that I began to sit down and pour my thoughts onto pages; some ended up thrown out, some ended up tear-stained, and some ended up in here.

I'm no poet, I never claimed to be, but if any of my words touch you or make you think, then I've achieved what I've always wanted to do.

I hope you all find your purpose and choose always to live and be all you can be.

-Me